WHAT'S THE CALL?

FROM THE PAGES OF
SPORTS ILLUSTRATED FOR KIDS MAGAZINE

A SPORTS ILLUSTRATED FOR KIDS BOOK

What's the Call? by SPORTS ILLUSTRATED FOR KIDS

A SPORTS ILLUSTRATED FOR KIDS publication/
February 1993 (revised January 2000)

SPORTS ILLUSTRATED FOR KIDS and **KiDS** are registered
trademarks of Time Inc.

Cover design by Emily Peterson Perez
Interior design by Miriam Dustin
Illustrations by Shannon Jeffries

What's the Call? is published by SPORTS ILLUSTRATED
FOR KIDS, a division of Time Inc. Its trademark is registered in the U.S. Patent and Trademark Office and
in other countries. SPORTS ILLUSTRATED FOR KIDS,
1271 Avenue of the Americas, New York, NY 10020

Printed in the United States of America
10 9 8 7 6 5 4 3 2

ISBN: 1-886749-84-1

What's the Call? is a production of
SPORTS ILLUSTRATED FOR KIDS Books

INTRODUCTION

Imagine that you are the umpire in a major league baseball game. What call would you make if the shortstop fielded a double-play grounder and then threw and hit the runner as he left first base? (See page 42 for answer.) Imagine that you are a referee in a youth basketball game. Two players collide under the basket. Is there a foul? If so, who gets the ball? These tough, split-second decisions are ones made every day by the officials, umpires, judges, and referees in the world of sports. As the referee or umpire, you are expected to watch all the action and know all the rules.

What's the Call? is an awesome way to test your knowledge of rules in 13 different sports, from baseball to basketball, from soccer to swimming. In *What's the Call?*, you are the official, umpire, or referee, so you wear the whistle. You must make the right call in 38 lively and fun sports situations — the teams and the players are depending on you!

Use *What's the Call?* to test yourself or to challenge your friends.

IS IT A TOUCHDOWN?

Central High quarterback Mike Clark is in trouble. His team has been pushed back to its own five-yard line. Now it is third down and 15 yards to go for a first down. Mike takes the snap from his center and drops back to pass from his own end zone. He is immediately surrounded by tacklers from Southern High's defense. Mike has no time to pass, so he tries to run. Crunch! Two line-backers tackle him in the end zone.

The referee blows his whistle and holds his hands above his head, palms together. Has a team scored? If so, which team? Is it a touchdown, a touchback, or a safety? How many points does that team receive?

DON'T GET PUSHY!

Patty Shea is starting in her first junior varsity volleyball game. Her team, Valley High, is playing Shamrock High, and Patty is nervous.

Valley High serves to begin the match, and the ball sails low over the net. A Shamrock player dives and gets her fists under the ball just before it hits the floor. The ball sails back over the net. Lucky save, Patty says to herself.

Oops! The ball is headed toward Patty, and she isn't ready as she stands flat-footed, with her hands at her sides. Patty does the only thing she can do: She swings underhand with both arms and slaps the ball with the palms of her hands.

The ball soars over the net and comes down on the Shamrock side. Patty is so happy with her hit that she doesn't notice that you, the referee, have blown your whistle to stop play. Why have you blown your whistle? What's your call?

BLOCK THAT SHOT!

The Windham Bulls are playing the Lake City Rustlers in a high school basketball game. With 10 seconds left, the Bulls trail by 2 points, 34-32.

Bulls guard Junior Jordan dribbles the ball up the court and then starts a drive toward the basket. At the foul line, Junior finds his path blocked by the Rustlers' 6'6" center, Carl Robinson. Time is running out, so Junior decides to take a jump shot. He leaps and raises the ball to shoot.

But Carl jumps, reaches out, and puts his hand on the ball before Junior can release it. The ball never leaves Junior's hands. Junior lands and notices that two seconds remain on the clock, so he throws up a quick shot before Carl can react. This time, the ball swishes through the hoop.

Junior thinks he has tied the score. But you are the referee, and you blew your whistle just as Junior launched his second shot. What's your call?

GET OUT OF THE WAY!

The Los Angeles Dodgers were leading the New York Yankees 3-1 in the fourth game of the 1978 World Series. The Yankees were batting in the sixth inning, and there was one out. Lou Piniella was at the plate. Thurman Munson was on second base and Reggie Jackson was on first.

Lou hit a line drive toward Dodger shortstop Bill Russell. The ball hit Bill's glove and popped out. Bill quickly picked up the ball and stepped on second base, forcing Reggie for one out. Bill then turned to throw to first base to try and get Lou and complete a double play. Reggie, who was running toward second base, stopped when he saw Bill step on second. Reggie didn't mean to block Bill's throw to first, but he did. Bill's throw hit him on the leg and bounced into foul territory as Lou raced across first base.

The Dodgers argued that both Reggie and Lou should be out because Reggie interfered with the throw to first. The umpire made his final ruling. What was it?

DOUBLE UP

Flora Fumbles has not been serving well in the city youth tennis tournament. She lost the first set of her opening match, 6-2, and she is serving to begin the second set.

When Flora serves, she likes to hold two tennis balls in her left hand and her racket in her right. If she botches her first serve attempt, she has another ball handy to use for her second serve.

This time, however, Flora accidentally tosses up both balls. One ball zips into the net, but the other one flies over it and lands in her opponent's service court. Flora's opponent is so confused that she lets the ball bounce past her without swinging at it.

You are the umpire, and you have a tough call to make. Has Flora served an ace?

HOCKEY HOME RUN

It is the last Bantam League hockey game of the winter, and Eagle defenseman Tank Martin is sad because he has never scored a goal. He sure would like to get at least one shot past an opposing goalie.

The Eagles are losing to the Robins, 5-1, with eight minutes left in the game. Tank hasn't given up. He steals the puck and takes off up the ice. Tank isn't a fast skater, but he is a smart one. He passes to high-scoring teammate Greg Gaskette, who takes a shot.

The puck bounces off the goalie's skate and flips into the air. The puck is about belly high, and it's sailing right toward Tank. Tank lifts his stick and swings it like a baseball bat. Crack! He hits the puck, and it sails over the goalie's shoulder, right into the net.

Is Tank's goal legal, or do you call him for high-sticking?

A REAL BELLYFUL

Gus Goon plays cornerback for the Grizzlies in a youth football league. The Grizzlies are losing 14-8 to the Bigfoots, and Gus is mad. On a third down play in the third quarter, Gus sees that the Bigfoots are running the ball in his direction. Gus is ready, and he tells himself that there is no way the Bigfoot runner is going to get past him.

Gus charges forward like a human cannonball. He bowls over one blocker and suddenly finds himself right in front of the Bigfoots' ballcarrier.

Gus puts his head down and — *whack!* — hits the runner in the belly with the top of his helmet. Gus wraps his arms around the ballcarrier's hips and drags him to the ground, right at the line of scrimmage.

You are the referee. As soon as the players hit the ground, you blow your whistle and throw your penalty flag. Why?

10

WATCH YOUR STEP

The score is tied 1-1 in a girls' soccer game between the Tigers and the Kickers.

Early in the second half, the Kickers' goaltender, Tina Lattery, makes a spectacular diving save just in front of her net. She quickly jumps to her feet with the ball in her hands and looks for a teammate to whom she can pass. Tina spots center Nina Goodwin on her left. As Tina winds up to throw, she takes a step backward, carrying the ball over the goal line between the goalposts.

The Tiger players immediately begin pointing at Tina. They say that by carrying the ball across the Kickers' goal line by mistake, she has scored the go-ahead goal for the Tigers! The Kickers claim the ball is still in play and that the score is still tied. What's your call?

HOLD STILL!

Claudia Rossi is swimming in the state championships for the first time. She has reached the final, and she will swim in the lane next to the defending state champ, Luci Filio.

Claudia is anxious, and when the starter shouts, "Take your marks," she bends down quickly and grabs the front of her starting block. She is ready to spring from the block as soon as she hears the starting gun.

Suddenly, out of the corner of her eye, Claudia sees Luci shift her weight. Claudia blasts off the block in reaction to the movement. As she hits the water, Claudia realizes the starter did not fire his gun. You're the starter, and you know that Claudia dived in because Luci moved. Do you disqualify Claudia for a false start? Do you disqualify Luci?

CAUGHT BY A FLY

With one out in the bottom of the sixth inning and his Little League team, the Spinners, behind 1-0, Glenn Jackson slugs a triple. Next up is cleanup hitter Peter White.

The pitcher for the Robots winds up and delivers. Peter times his swing perfectly and — *crack!* — the ball soars like a rocket toward centerfield.

Glenn leaves third base instantly and sprints toward home. As he crosses the plate, he throws up his arms to celebrate, thinking he has scored the tying run. Meanwhile, the Robots centerfielder goes back, back, back, back . . . and makes a great catch! Peter is out. The Robots third baseman yells for the ball. The centerfielder fires it to the shortstop, who relays the ball to third. The third baseman catches the ball and steps on the base.

Now the Robots are celebrating, but why? You are the umpire. What's the call?

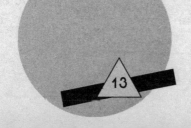

BALANCING ACT

Yolanda Steptoe is competing in a kids' gymnastics meet. It's her turn to perform a routine on the balance beam.

Yolanda goes smoothly through her routine until she gets to one of her last tricks, a cartwheel. Yolanda finishes swinging her feet over her head when she loses her balance. She thinks she is going to fall off, but she twists around and lands sitting on the beam. Yolanda stands and completes her routine. "Whew," Yolanda thinks to herself after her dismount. "I'll get a slightly lower score because of that mistake, but at least I didn't fall to the ground. That would have cost me an extra five tenths [.5] of a point." You are the judge. You do deduct .5 of a point for the fall, even though Yolanda did not fall to the ground. Why?

JUMPING JIMMY!

It's late in the fourth quarter of a Pee Wee basketball game, and the Blazers lead the Kings, 60-48. Jimmy Cricket, a reserve forward for the Blazers, has just entered the game. He takes up his position near the base of the foul line. Blazer guard Sam Connors brings the ball down on Jimmy's side of the court, and bounces a nifty pass to Jimmy.

Jimmy takes a couple of dribbles to his right and stops. He jumps to shoot, but his defender jumps too. So Jimmy changes his mind and comes down without taking a shot. He jumps again, shoots, and . . . scores!

Jimmy thinks he has just scored his first 2 points of the season. But you are the referee and you know better. You blow your whistle, stopping the Blazers' wild cheering. What's your call?

POINT OR NO POINT?

The Springers lead the Eagles 14-13 in the deciding game of an important volleyball match. The Springers need just one point to win the championship!

Kelly Gooding of the Eagles is serving. She hits the ball high over the net to Sherry Edwards, who is playing in the front row for the Springers. Sherry "bumps" the ball to teammate Karen Shoe, and Karen pounds it over the net.

Toni Clark of the Eagles dives for the ball, but it bounces off her arm and sails out-of-bounds.

The Springers jump up and down in celebration. They think they've won the match. You are the referee and you know better. You point toward the Springers' side of the court.

What's your call?

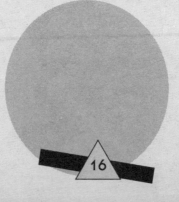

THE SEAT OF HIS PANTS

In July 1988, Mike Conley was competing at the United States Olympic trials. He was trying out for the track and field team in the triple jump event. To get a spot on the team, Mike needed to finish in first, second, or third place.

At the trials, each competitor was allowed six jumps. On Mike's fifth jump, he sailed 57 feet 9 3/4 inches to move into third place. But by the final round, Mike had slipped to fourth place. To make the team, he needed to jump at least 57 feet 10 1/4 inches on his final try.

Mike sped down the runway and took off. His heels landed 57 feet 11 1/4 inches from the takeoff board, good enough for third place and a spot on the Olympic team!

But you were judging the event. When Mike landed, you noticed that his shorts touched the sand behind his feet, at 57 feet 7 inches. It's your call: Did Mike make the Olympic team?

WINDMILL WINDUP

Jenny Hawkins is pitching for the Rangers in a slo-pitch softball game. Her team is leading the Bears 1-0. The bases are loaded, and Colleen McNulty is at the plate. The count is three balls and two strikes, and there are two outs.

Jenny wants to strike out Colleen, so she decides to try out her secret weapon: the Hawkins windmill special. Jenny begins her windmill windup. She swings her pitching

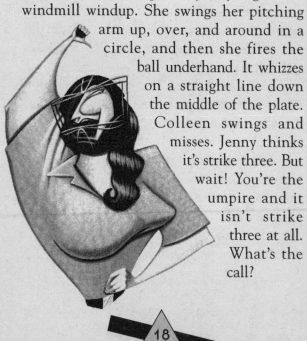

arm up, over, and around in a circle, and then she fires the ball underhand. It whizzes on a straight line down the middle of the plate. Colleen swings and misses. Jenny thinks it's strike three. But wait! You're the umpire and it isn't strike three at all. What's the call?

WHAT'S THE CATCH?

The Oakland Raiders were leading the Pittsburgh Steelers 7-6 with 22 seconds left in a 1972 American Football Conference playoff game. The Steelers had the ball on their own 40-yard line, and it was fourth down and 10 yards to go for a first down.

Pittsburgh quarterback Terry Bradshaw dropped back to pass. He saw running back Frenchy Fuqua open about 25 yards downfield, and he fired. Before the ball reached Frenchy, though, Oakland safety Jack Tatum got in the way. The ball bounced off one of Jack's shoulder pads and flew about seven yards back toward the line of scrimmage, right to Steelers' rookie running back Franco Harris.

Franco caught the ball at the 42-yard line and ran all the way for a touchdown. The Steelers were sure they had won the playoff game, but the Oakland players claimed that Franco's catch was illegal. You were the referee. Did the Steelers' touchdown count? What was your call?

STEADY AS A ROCK

The Plymouth Rocks and the Columbus Explorers are tied, with 30 seconds left in a girls' basketball game. The Rocks have the ball, and they pass it to May Flower, their star center, for the final shot.

With 10 seconds remaining, May, who is standing near the baseline, dribbles twice, then takes a 10-foot jump shot. May is nervous, so her aim is off target. Clunk! The ball hits the side of the backboard and bounces straight back to her. The clock is ticking, so May quickly puts up another shot. This time, the ball swishes through the hoop just as the horn sounds to end the game.

May and her teammates are excited. But the Explorers say May's basket shouldn't count because her first shot hit the side of the backboard. You're the referee. What do you say?

HELPING HAND

The action is red hot between the Flames and the Boilers in a Bantam League hockey game. With only two minutes left, the score is 2-2.

Sparky Wood, a Flames forward, has just taken two shots on goal. Both times, Boilers goalie Sonny Burns blocked the puck. If Sparky can get one more chance, the Flames know he'll slap the winning goal right past Sonny.

Yes! Sparky steals the puck and charges up the ice again. He cocks his stick, swings, and — *crack!* — his stick smashes against the ice and breaks. Sparky drops his stick and kicks the puck toward a teammate. Another Flame player rushes to the bench, grabs a new stick, and throws it to Sparky. You blow your whistle and charge the Flames with a two-minute penalty.

Why?

STROKE SWITCH

Randi Float is ready to dive into the pool as soon as she hears the starter's gun. It's Randi's first swim meet, and she is competing in the 100-meter freestyle event for kids 11 and 12 years old.

On your marks! Get set! Bang!

Randi is off quickly. She swims the crawl stroke for one length of the 50-meter pool and is in the lead when she turns at the halfway point.

With 26 meters to go, Randi is out of breath and her arms hurt because she has been swimming so fast. She doesn't want to quit, though, so she switches to the breaststroke, takes a few gulps of air, and then starts swimming the crawl again.

Although doing the breaststroke slowed her down, Randi still touches the wall in third place, which is good enough to earn her a ribbon. However, a swimmer from another team says Randi should be disqualified because she switched strokes. What's the call?

ALL CAUGHT UP

Terry Mullholland of the San Francisco Giants was pitching against the New York Mets in a 1986 game. Terry was just a rookie that season, and he was struggling. In the first two innings, Terry walked five batters and gave up two runs.

In the third inning, Keith Hernandez batted for the Mets. Terry fired a pitch, and Keith smashed a hard grounder between the pitcher's mound and first base. Terry raced off the mound, stuck out his glove, and snared the ball.

Terry tried to take the ball from his glove and flip it to the first baseman for the out. But the ball wouldn't budge. Terry was using a new glove, and the ball had become stuck in it.

Terry took a few steps toward first base and yanked off his glove with the ball still wedged inside. He tossed the ball with the glove to first baseman Bob Brenly. Bob caught the glove before Keith crossed the first base bag. Was Keith out or was he safe?

THE BOUNCING BALL

Twelve-year-old Kim Chou is competing in a junior bowling tournament. She's on a roll: In the fifth of 10 frames, she earned a spare by knocking down all 10 pins with two rolls of her ball. In the sixth frame, she knocked all the pins down with one ball for her first-ever strike!

Now Kim is ready to roll for the second time in the seventh frame. Three pins are still standing. Kim takes her three-step approach and swings the ball forward.

The approach is perfect but Kim's thumb catches in the thumbhole as she releases the ball. The ball is jerked to one side. It bounces in the lane and then into the gutter. But this is Kim's lucky game. The ball hits the edge of the gutter, pops back into the lane, and knocks over the three remaining pins.

"Awesome!" Kim shouts. She has rolled another spare!

But you are the scorekeeper and you give Kim credit for only knocking down seven pins, not all 10. Why?

ROLLING ALONG

Morris Knight is huge! The starting center on the Dewitt High School basketball team is 6'6" tall. Tonight, Dewitt is playing Lee High School. Lee High's center, Jerome Nelson, is only 5'11".

Early in the game, the ball bounces off the knee of a Dewitt player and rolls out-of-bounds. Jerome takes the ball to throw it in for Lee High. Big Morris is standing in front of Jerome, waving his arms. Jerome is tricky, though. He spots teammate Tim Bass standing 10 feet behind Morris. Jerome rolls the ball right between Morris's legs, straight to Tim!

Tim picks up the ball and goes in for a layup.

Morris is furious. He says the basket shouldn't count because Jerome rolled the ball into play. What do you say?

A WEIRD SPIN

Steffi Graf and Martina Navratilova were playing in the final tennis match of a major professional tennis event. It was Martina's serve, and she hit the ball low and hard. Steffi hit a powerful return shot, and the ball landed right at Martina's feet. Martina reacted quickly. She flicked the ball with her racket and sent it looping into the air. The ball sailed just over the net and landed on Steffi's side of the court.

Steffi charged forward, and it looked as if she would be able to reach the ball easily. But Martina had put so much backspin on the ball that when it hit the court, the ball bounced *backward*, toward Martina. Before Steffi could touch it, the ball spun back over the net and landed on Martina's side of the court. You were the umpire. Who won the point?

CHEST SHOT

Emilio Garcia and Rocky Blades are teammates on the Spring Lake Junior High School soccer team.

Spring Lake is playing a team from Belmar. Emilio gets control of the ball. Rocky is a few yards away, and the two begin an awesome display of passing and dribbling the ball as they move down the field.

When they are within shooting distance of the Belmar goal, Rocky runs to the right side of the field. He stays parallel with Emilio so he won't be called for offside. Emilio dribbles to the left side of the goal. He fakes a shot to draw out the goalie, then kicks the ball into the air toward Rocky, who expects to head the ball into the goal.

Emilio's timing is perfect, but his aim is off. The ball sails toward Rocky at shoulder level, not head level. Rocky swings his body and hits the ball with his chest into the net. Goal!

The Belmar players protest that Rocky hit the ball illegally because he used his chest to shoot the ball. You are the referee. What's your call?

WATCH YOUR FEET

Heidi Beatty is competing in a high school gymnastics meet. She is performing her new floor exercise routine for the first time.

Heidi's first moves are three cartwheels in a row, and she hits them perfectly. She bounces from her feet to a handstand, then does a split. So far, so good.

Heidi knows she is doing well, and for a moment she imagines herself scoring a 9.9 and winning an Olympic gold medal!

Oops! On a front walkover, Heidi steps over the line at the edge of the exercise area. She pulls her foot back quickly and hopes the judges did not notice her error.

You are one of the judges, though, and you did notice that she stepped out of bounds. Should Heidi be disqualified?

THE BIG BOUNCE

It's late in a football game between the Mudhens and the Razorbacks. The Mudhens have been ahead 13-12 since the second quarter, but the Razorbacks hope that the score is about to change. They have the ball on the Mudhens eight-yard line. It's fourth and goal-to-go, and the Razorbacks are lined up for a field goal. The Razorbacks' kicker is Chad Foote, and their holder is Aaron Finger.

Aaron catches the snap from the center and sets up the ball for the kick. Chad's kick sails high toward the left goalpost.

Thwack! The ball hits the upright part of the goalpost and bounces back toward the playing field. Aaron catches it before it hits the ground, and he scoots into the end zone.

His teammates are jumping up and down. They think it's a touchdown. You're the referee. What's your call?

RELAY RACE CHASE

Nicki Shea is running the third leg of the 4 x 100-meter relay for the Striders Track Club. Nicki leads the race, but now she must pass the baton to Sharon Reed, who will run the final leg.

Sharon stands just inside the exchange zone, an area 22 yards long in which the baton must be passed from runner to runner. Sharon begins running just before Nicki arrives with the baton. But Sharon takes off too quickly. Her right foot is out of the exchange zone when she reaches back into the zone and takes the baton. Sharon then zooms away and finishes first.

The Striders think they've won the relay. The other teams argue that Sharon was out of the exchange zone. The Striders say that doesn't matter because *the baton* was in the zone when it was passed. What's the call?

RUNDOWN

Randy Fleetfoot is on third base. His team, the Cougars, is losing to the Monarchs, 7-6, in the sixth inning of a Little League game. Randy is the tying run.

The batter hits a hot grounder between the shortstop and the third baseman, and Randy breaks for home. But the Monarch shortstop fields the ball and fires to the catcher.

Randy is halfway home when he sees that the catcher is standing on the plate holding the ball. Uh-oh! Randy turns around and heads back toward third. The catcher throws the ball to his third baseman. Now Randy is caught in a rundown.

Randy has to turn around again and run for home. Unfortunately, the catcher has sneaked up the foul line behind him. When Randy turns — *slam!* — he runs right into the catcher. Both players tumble to the ground. Randy gets up and tries to score, but the third baseman tags him out.

Is Randy out, or does he score because the catcher got in his way in the baseline? You are the home-plate ump. What's your call?

SIDE POCKET

Jane Friedmann is playing a game of eight ball in the Livermore Billiards Tournament. She has knocked all of the striped balls into the pockets. To win the game, all she has to do is choose a pocket, tell the judge what pocket she is aiming for, and knock the black eight ball into that pocket.

Jane studies the table. The eight ball is right next to the side pocket. "This will be a breeze!" Jane tells herself. She calls her shot, quickly lines it up, and hits the white cue ball toward the eight ball.

Oops! Jane should have taken her time. The cue ball rolls across the table and just nicks the eight ball. The eight ball gently bounces off the side cushion and rolls to a stop. But the cue ball bounces off the side cushion, rolls back across the table, and drops into the other side pocket!

You are the tournament judge. What happens next?

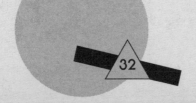

AN ICY SITUATION

It's a youth hockey game between the Flyers and the Blue Angels. Center Pat Graystone of the Flyers brings the puck across the blue line and into the team's offensive zone. He passes to a wing, gets the puck back, and passes again. Bobby Shott, a Blue Angels' defenseman, intercepts the pass. Bobby slaps the puck down the ice, and it thumps against the boards at the opposite end.

Players from both teams race for the puck. You are there too, because you are the referee. Pat reaches the puck first, and as soon as he touches it, you blow the whistle. What's your call?

33

LOSING CONTROL

Andy Swenson is competing in a slalom race for boys ages 10 to 12. In the slalom event, one skier at a time races down a course marked with gates, which are poles stuck in the snow. Each skier must weave back and forth around the gates as he goes down the hill. The skier with the fastest time wins.

Andy blasts out of the starting block and rockets down the hill. He skis around the first gate. Swoosh. He skis around the second. Swoosh.

Andy weaves around all of the gates perfectly. All he has to do is zip straight down the last 30 yards of the course.

Oops! Andy hits a bump and flies into the air. He swings his arms wildly to keep his balance. Andy lands hard, and one of his skis pops off. Somehow, he keeps from falling down and crosses the finish line on one ski.

Andy's time is the fastest of the day. You are the finish line judge. Does he win the gold medal, or is he disqualified for losing a ski?

SUPER PLAY

It's January 22, 1989, and you're the referee at Super Bowl XXIII, in Miami. The San Francisco 49ers trail the Cincinnati Bengals 13-6 at the start of the fourth quarter.

The 49ers have driven all the way to Cincinnati's 14-yard line. Quarterback Joe Montana drops back to pass. He spots wide receiver Jerry Rice near the left sideline, and throws. Jerry catches the ball at the two-yard line, takes a step toward the goal line, and is knocked out-of-bounds. But as he flies through the air, Jerry extends the ball with one arm so that it crosses the goal line and passes through a corner of the end zone.

The 49ers think it's a touchdown. The Bengals say no way. You're right there. What's your call! Remember, the Super Bowl may be at stake!

ALLEY-OOPS!

North High School is playing South High School in a girls' basketball game. The score is tied with only three seconds left. South High has the ball out-of-bounds near the half-court line.

Claire Booth and her South High teammates try a special play. As soon as the referee hands the ball to Claire to throw inbounds, Claire's teammate Rosanne Franklin breaks for the basket. Claire lobs an alley-oop pass toward the basket. Roseanne plans to jump up and tip the ball in to win the game.

At the last instant, though, Roseanne realizes that Claire's pass is too high for her to reach. The ball hits the backboard without being touched and goes into the basket! Roseanne and her teammates rush over to slap high fives with Claire. They think that she has scored the game-winner.

You're the referee, and you have blown your whistle. What call do you make?

HOT DOG

It's the bottom of the ninth inning in a minor league baseball game between the Pickles and the Mustards. The Pickles shortstop is named Frank Footer, but people call him Hot Dog.

Hot Dog has been on a roll. He has driven in three runs and made some slick catches. The Pickles lead 6-4. Hot Dog doesn't think the Mustards can catch up, even though they have runners on first and second base. There are two outs.

Batting for the Mustards is Red Relish. The count is one ball and one strike. The next pitch to Red is over the outside corner of the plate, and Red swings. *Ping!* Red hits a pop fly into shallow leftfield. Hot Dog yells "Mine!" as he runs into position to make the catch.

Hot Dog figures he will catch the ball easily, so he decides to show off. As the ball is coming, Hot Dog removes his cap and holds it out. The ball drops right into the cap. Hot Dog thinks the inning and the game are over, and he trots off the field. You're the umpire, though, and you make another call. What is it?

37

A SWING AND A MISS

Kitty Katt is serving for her seventh-grade volleyball team in a game against the eighth-graders. Kitty's team leads 13-12 in the third game of a best-of-three match.

Kitty is nervous. Her coach taught her to throw the ball into the air and swing her arm around to hit it. Kitty holds the ball in her left hand and makes a fist with her right. She looks across the court and then at the ball. After taking a deep breath, she tosses the ball straight up, swings her arm around, and . . . misses the ball completely! It bounces off the floor and Kitty catches it. A couple of eighth-graders laugh. How embarrassing, Kitty thinks. What happens next?

TOUCHDOWN!

Bruce Lee is set to kick a field goal for the Raiders in their college football game with the Ducks. The ball is on the 35-yard line. Bruce will be kicking from the 42. The goalpost is at the back of the end zone, 10 yards behind the goal line, so this will be a 52-yard attempt.

The ball is snapped to the holder, who sets it up for the kick. Bruce steps forward and kicks the ball. Whack!

At that moment, a Ducks linebacker plows through the line. He throws up his arms, and his right hand nicks the ball. Instead of sailing high and far toward the goalpost, the ball flutters low in the air.

Tommy Swan is standing on the Ducks' 20-yard line. He catches the ball and takes off for the opposite goal line, 80 yards away. Tommy can really fly, and he glides all the way into the end zone.

You are an official and you must make a call. Does the TD count, or does the ball go back to the 20-yard line, where Tommy caught it?

DOES SHE NEED A HAND?

A soccer game between the Clippers and the Blue Streaks is tied 2-2. Amy Grant, a midfielder for the Clippers, dribbles the ball across the center line and waits for her teammates to get into position. Amy darts to her right to start a play and spots an open teammate, Tracy Long, streaking toward the goal.

Amy kicks her pass over Tracy's head. So Tracy, who is new at the game, jumps and catches the ball with both hands. She drops it and kicks it past the startled Blue Streak goalie for the go-ahead score.

You blow your whistle and make a chopping motion with one hand against the other. What's your call?

HAMMER TIME

First baseman Kirk Hammer has belted a lot of hits this season for his minor league baseball team, the Oakland C's. But today, Kirk can't do anything right. He hasn't had a hit, and the C's are trailing the Giants, 2-0, in the bottom of the ninth inning. Kirk steps up to the plate with one out and nobody on base. The fans cheer loudly for their favorite slugger!

The Giants pitcher fires and Kirk takes a hack — and misses the pitch. Strike 1. The same thing happens with the second pitch. Strike 2. The third pitch is low and outside, but Kirk takes another wild swing at it anyway, and misses. Strike 3.

After that last swing, though, Kirk sees the ball skip past the catcher and roll toward the backstop. Kirk drops his bat and sprints to first base. By the time the catcher has retrieved the ball, Kirk is already standing on the bag.

You're the umpire. Why is Kirk on first base if he just struck out?

41

ANSWERS

IS IT A TOUCHDOWN? Southern scored a safety, which is worth two points. The defensive team scores a safety when it tackles a man trying to carry the ball out of his own end zone.

DON'T GET PUSHY! You call Patty for "lifting" the ball. This call is made when a player hits the ball upward with the palms of her hands. A player must hit the ball with her forearms, the heels of her hands, or her fists. You award the service to Shamrock High.

BLOCK THAT SHOT! The basket does not count. You call a jump ball between Junior and Carl because both players had possession — a firm hold on the ball — at the same time.

GET OUT OF THE WAY! A runner who is forced out can't intentionally block a throw. If he does, the batter or runner is out at the base where the throw was going before it was blocked. In this case, the umpire ruled that Reggie interfered accidentally. Lou was safe at first and Thurman scored.

DOUBLE UP Flora has not served an ace. The server is not allowed to throw more than one ball into the air at a time. You call a let, which means that Flora gets to try her first serve again.

HOCKEY HOME RUN The goal counts. A player may swing at the puck as long as the puck is below shoulder level. But if he hits another player with his stick, he will be called for high-sticking.

A REAL BELLYFUL You call a penalty on Gus for "spearing." It is illegal for a tackler to drive into a

ballcarrier with the top of his helmet. This rule protects the ballcarrier and the tackler from serious injury. Gus's team is penalized 15 yards.

WATCH YOUR STEP Tina did score the go-ahead goal for the Tigers when she stepped over the goal line. In soccer, a goalie may score a goal for the other team if she touches the ball while she is behind the goal line and between the goalposts.

HOLD STILL! Claudia is not disqualified because she started in reaction to Luci's motion. Swimmers in the ready position must remain still. If you, as the official, think Luci moved on purpose to make Claudia start early, you disqualify Luci. If it was an accident, you give Luci a warning.

CAUGHT BY A FLY Glenn is out, the game is over, and the Robots win. Glenn forgot to "tag up." A base runner may not advance on a fly out until the ball has been caught. A runner who leaves early is out as soon as his base is touched by an opposing player holding the ball. Glenn should have waited until the ball was caught to leave for home.

BALANCING ACT On the beam, a gymnast loses five tenths (.5) of a point for falling, even if she lands on the beam and doesn't fall to the ground. For Yolanda's fall, you would deduct an additional .1 to .3 of a point because Yolanda failed to execute the trick properly. This is called an execution error.

JUMPING JIMMY! Jimmy is guilty of traveling. The basket does not count, and the ball goes to the Kings. A player travels when he jumps and lands while holding the ball. (Traveling is also called

when a player advances more than a step without dribbling, or when he moves his pivot foot.) Jimmy should have shot or passed the ball while he was in the air.

POINT OR NO POINT? In volleyball, only the team that is serving may score. The Springers did not score the winning point. You, the referee, are signaling a "side out" to the Springers. It's their serve, and they can win the match if they win the next point.

THE SEAT OF HIS PANTS Mike's final jump was 57 feet 7 inches, and he did not qualify for the team. Track-and-field rules state that a jump is measured from the takeoff board to the closest point at which a jumper's body or uniform touches the sand.

WINDMILL WINDUP You call ball four because Jenny threw an illegal pitch. Colleen trots to first base, the runners advance one base, and the tying run scores. In slo-pitch softball, a pitcher is not allowed to wind up with a full windmill. Also, a pitched ball must arc to a height between 6 and 12 feet before dropping across the plate. Jenny's special pitch broke both rules.

WHAT'S THE CATCH? The touchdown counted, Pittsburgh won, and Franco's catch became known as the Immaculate Reception. If one of Franco's teammates had deflected the ball, the pass would have been incomplete. The NFL changed this rule in 1978. The new rule allows a receiver to catch a pass after the ball has deflected off a defensive or an offensive player.

STEADY AS A ROCK May's basket counts, and the Rocks win the game. The sides of the backboard are considered inbounds. A ball that hits the side of the backboard is still in play.

HELPING HAND The Flames are penalized because a player threw a stick to Sparky. There would not have been a penalty if the player had handed him the stick. The two-minute penalty can be served by any Flames player.

STROKE SWITCH Randi is not disqualified for switching from the crawl to the breaststroke. Swimmers in the freestyle event are allowed to swim any stroke they choose. Most choose the crawl, the fastest stroke.

ALL CAUGHT UP Keith is out. On a play at first base or a force play at any base, the runner is out if the fielder has the ball and touches the bag before the runner reaches the base. It doesn't matter if the ball is in another player's glove.

THE BOUNCING BALL A ball is dead as soon as it goes into the gutter. It is considered a gutter ball even if it bounces out and knocks over some pins. If the ball had bounced out of the gutter on the first ball of the frame, Kim would have had to reset the pins before rolling her second ball.

ROLLING ALONG The basket does not count. Morris is right! According to high school rules, a player is not allowed to roll the ball on a throw-in. The ball must be bounced or thrown. Dewitt gets the ball out-of-bounds.

A WEIRD SPIN Martina won the point because

Steffi failed to hit a ball that landed in her court. Steffi eventually won the match.

CHEST SHOT Rocky's goal is good. A soccer player can hit, pass, or shoot the ball with any part of the body except the hands and arms.

WATCH YOUR FEET Heidi is not disqualified for stepping out of bounds. However, stepping over the line is considered a "deduction" in her routine. As a judge, you take one tenth of a point off her score.

THE BIG BOUNCE It's not a touchdown. The play was dead when the ball hit the goalpost and bounced back toward the playing field. The play is ruled as a missed field goal attempt, and the Mudhens get the ball at their own 20-yard line. If the ball had hit the goalpost and gone over the crossbar, the field goal would have counted.

RELAY RACE CHASE The Striders have won the race and the city title. Track rules state that the baton must be within the exchange zone when it is passed from one runner to the next.

At the 1988 Summer Olympics, the U.S. men's 4 x 100-meter relay team, which was favored to win the gold medal, was disqualified because they made one exchange while the baton was completely out of the zone.

RUNDOWN You call Randy safe at home. The catcher is guilty of obstruction, or getting in the way. A defensive player is not allowed to stand in the base path and interfere with a base runner unless the defensive player has the ball. If the defensive player gets in the way of a base runner,

the runner is allowed to take the base he was running toward. In this case, the base was home plate.

SIDE POCKET The game is over, and Jane loses. A player must not scratch (knock the cue ball into a pocket) while trying to sink the eight ball. Jane should have hit the cue ball softly so that, even if she had missed her shot, the cue ball would have stopped before it rolled across the table.

AN ICY SITUATION You call the Blue Angels for icing the puck. You bring the puck back to their defensive zone for a face-off.

Icing occurs when a player shoots the puck from one end of the ice to the other and a member of the opposing team is the first player to touch it after it crosses the goal line. Icing, however, cannot be charged to a team that is short-handed.

LOSING CONTROL Andy wins the gold medal because a skier is permitted to cross the finish line while wearing only one ski. The skier must wear both skis while weaving around the gates on the course.

SUPER PLAY It's a touchdown! NFL rules state that a touchdown is scored when the ball crosses the goal line while it is in a player's possession. The player's body need not cross the line. If Jerry had hit the ground out-of-bounds before the ball crossed the goal line, the touchdown would not have counted. The 49ers won, 20-16.

ALLEY-OOPS! You rule that the basket does not count, so the South team has not won the game. A ball thrown in from out-of-bounds is not in play

until another player touches it. North gets possession of the ball at the spot where Claire threw it inbounds. There are still three seconds remaining in the game.

HOT DOG You signal an illegal catch because a fielder is not allowed to catch a fair or foul ball with his cap, mask, or any other piece of equipment or clothing. Each runner advances three bases. This means the two Mustard base runners score to tie the game and Red goes to third base. There are still two outs.

A SWING AND A MISS Kitty gets one more chance to serve. If she takes longer than five seconds or misses again, a side out is called and the serve goes to the other team.

TOUCHDOWN! You signal a touchdown for the Ducks. A player is permitted to run back field-goal attempts just as he is allowed to run back punts and kickoffs.

DOES SHE NEED A HAND? Tracy has illegally handled the ball. Only goalies are allowed to touch the ball intentionally with their hands or arms. Tracy intentionally used her hands when she caught the ball, so the Blue Streaks are awarded a direct kick from the spot of the infraction.

HAMMER TIME If the catcher doesn't catch strike three, the batter can run to first base as long as there are fewer than two outs and no runner is on first. The batter is out if the catcher throws to first before the batter gets there. This rule is not used in youth leagues.